Jaguars

Jaguars

Theresa Woods

THE CHILD'S WORLD®, INC.

Published in the United States of America by The Child's World®, Inc.
PO Box 326
Chanhassen, MN 55317-0326
800-599-READ
www.childsworld.com

Product Manager Mary Berendes
Editor Katherine Stevenson
Designer Mary Berendes
Contributor Bob Temple

Photo Credits
© 2001 Alejandro Balaguer/Stone: 19
ANIMALS ANIMALS © Dani/Jeske: 9
ANIMALS ANIMALS © Erwin & Peggy Bauer: 6
ANIMALS ANIMALS © Fabio Colombini: 2
ANIMALS ANIMALS © Gerard Lacz: 15, 20, 23, 24
ANIMALS ANIMALS © Lynn Stone: 13, 16
© Kenneth W. Fink, The National Audubon Society Collection/Photo Researchers: 29
© 1997 Kevin Schafer: 30
© 1998 Kevin Schafer: 10
© 2001 Renee Lynn/Stone: cover, 26

Library of Congress Cataloging-in-Publication Data
Woods, Theresa.
Jaguars / by Theresa Woods.
p. cm.
Includes index.
ISBN 1-56766-885-2 (library bound : alk. paper)
1. Jaguar—Juvenile literature. [1. Jaguar.]   I. Title.
QL737.C23 W664 2001
599.75'5—dc21
00-010770

On the cover...

Front cover: This jaguar is snarling at the photographer.
Page 2: This beautiful jaguar lives in the jungle in Brazil.

Table of Contents

Late afternoon sunlight breaks through the thick Amazon rain forest. Shadows spread across the jungle floor. A deer moves into the shadows, looking for food. As the deer passes, one of the shadows begins to move. The shadow creeps closer and closer. Finally, the shadowy animal leaps onto the deer and kills it with one bite. What type of creature is this? It's one of nature's most exciting animals. It's a jaguar!

What Do Jaguars Look Like?

Jaguars belong to a group of animals called **mammals.** Mammals have hair on their bodies and produce milk to feed their young. Cows, dogs, and lions are mammals, and so are people.

In its shape, the jaguar looks like a small tiger—but it has spots instead of stripes. Its body is about six feet long, with a long tail. It has a large, broad face with a wide nose and small ears that stand straight up. Jaguars are very powerfully built. They have a heavy body, a large chest, and short, well-muscled legs.

This adult jaguar lives in a South American jungle. ⇒

Jaguars are the largest type of wild cat found in North and South America. An adult female weighs about 175 pounds. An adult male can weigh up to 250 pounds! Only the lions and tigers of Africa and Asia are bigger.

A jaguar's most famous feature is its thick, beautiful fur. The jaguar is covered with golden brown fur that has black rings with small black spots in the center. (Leopards look like jaguars except that their rings don't have black spots.) Some jaguars are all black, and you can see their spots only in bright sunlight.

You can easily see this jaguar's beautiful spots ⇒
as it walks through a forest in Belize.

Where Do Jaguars Live?

A few jaguars have been seen in the wooded mountains of Arizona and New Mexico, but most live in South America. Many animals can live in only one type of environment, or **habitat.** Jaguars, however, can live in a wide range of habitats. They are found in thick forests, swampy grasslands, and even dry mountains. The best place to find jaguars, however, is in the dense rain forests of the Amazon Basin.

Jaguars like the water and are very good swimmers. They often live near lakes or rivers. To find enough food, an adult jaguar might claim a **territory,** or living space, of up to 25 square miles.

This adult has made its home next to a waterfall deep in the jungle. ⇒

Jaguars tend to be **nocturnal,** or most active at night. Sometimes, however, they are active in the early morning or around sunset. During the heat of the day, jaguars sleep or sun themselves on rocks.

What Do Jaguars Eat?

Jaguars are excellent **predators,** or hunters. The jaguar's beautiful spots act as **camouflage** to keep the animal hidden. Staying hidden, the jaguar slowly stalks its prey. When it is close enough, it jumps on the animal. It kills its prey by biting through the skull with one bite.

This jaguar is hard to see as it hunts in a jungle in Peru. ⇒

Jaguars catch and eat almost anything. They hunt monkeys and birds in tree branches. In the water, they catch fish, turtles, and even large alligator-like reptiles. However, they are best at catching land animals. Deer, armadillos, wild pigs, and large rodents all are prey for jaguars. A jaguar can kill some of these smaller animals just by slapping them with its powerful paw.

⇐ Here a young jaguar has caught a large fish to eat.

What Are Baby Jaguars Like?

Jaguars like to live alone. The only time jaguars get together is to mate. After mating, the male and female jaguar separate. Three months later, the female gives birth to about two babies.

At birth, the young jaguars are blind and drink only their mother's milk. After about three months, they can eat solid food and go with their mother on hunting trips. The young jaguars stay with their mother, learning to hunt and survive, until they are two years old. In the wild, jaguars can live to be about 20 years old.

Jaguar mothers like this one take good care of their babies. ⇒

Like most big cats, jaguars have no natural enemies, except people. The most serious threat to jaguars is the loss of their habitat. As people move into the jungles to live and farm, they destroy the forests and other places where the jaguars find their food.

⇐ By putting its ears back and showing its teeth, this jaguar is showing that it is angry.

People also sometimes kill the animals jaguars need for food. With both people and jaguars hunting the same animals, sometimes there is not enough food to go around.

Jaguars have been hunted to make their beautiful fur into coats, too. Most countries have tried to stop the hunting of jaguars, but illegal hunters called **poachers** still kill many jaguars every year.

Are Jaguars in Danger?

Jaguars are **endangered,** which means that they are in danger of dying out completely. Jaguars are hard to find and count in the wild, so scientists aren't sure how many are left. They estimate that there might be as few as 15,000 wild jaguars in the world.

You can see the spots on this black jaguar ⇒ when the sunlight hits its fur just right.

People in many countries, including Mexico, Brazil, and Costa Rica, are working to save the jaguar. They are trying to protect the jaguar's habitat and stop the hunting of jaguars for their fur. Many zoos are also trying to breed jaguars to increase their numbers. If this hard work pays off, jaguars will continue to roam free for years to come.

Glossary

camouflage (KAM-oo-flahj)
Camouflage is coloring or markings that help an animal blend into its surroundings. The jaguar's spots act as camouflage to help it hide.

endangered (en-DANE-jerd)
An endangered animal is one that is close to dying out completely. Jaguars are endangered.

habitat (HAB-ih-tat)
An animal's habitat is the type of area in which it lives. Jaguars can live in a wide range of habitats.

mammals (MAM-mullz)
Mammals are animals that have warm blood, have hair on their bodies, and feed their young milk from their bodies. Jaguars are mammals, and so are people.

nocturnal (nock-TURN-ull)
A nocturnal animal is active at night and sleeps during the day. Jaguars are mostly nocturnal.

poachers (POH-cherz)
Poachers are people who kill animals illegally. Poachers have killed many jaguars for their beautiful fur.

predators (PRED-uh-terz)
A predator is an animal that hunts and kills other animals for food. Jaguars are predators.

territory (TEHR-ih-tor-ee)
A territory is an area of land that an animal claims as its own. Each jaguar has its own territory.

Web Sites

http://dialspace.dial.pipex.com/agarman/jaguar.htm

http://www.primenet.com/~brendel/jaguar.html

http://www.thewildones.org/Animals/jaguar.html